A PRINCESS WHISPERS TO HER FATHER

Soleil C. Meade

Monda,
Such a sweet genuine person—
I pray this book encourages
+ helps you ♡ Enjoy love,
Soleil

Copyright © 2013 Soleil Meade

Victorious Life Media,
Columbia, MD
www.victoriouslifemedia.com

Book Production
First Edition Printing - February 2013

Editing: Jamie Fleming
Cover Design: Soleil Meade
Page Layout Design by Daniel Yeager- Nu-Image Design

ISBN 13: 978-0-9859554-2-7
ISBN 10: 0985955422

Printed in the United States of America

Introduction

His Kingdom is made of power, His castle's foundations are

righteousness and just

The tower I reside in is built of virtue, grace and trust.

He places a crown of glory on my head, and I bow.

In the presence of my Father, I receive my royal crown.

Son of God came to Earth, To die upon the cross

Warred in the enemy's camp, Conquered death for us all.

He rose with all power, Seated on the throne

The King is my Father, I am His princess, He whispers…

Daughter, You Are My Own

Table of Contents

Establishing The Princess
Chapter 1
Accepting Your Royal Crown

Many of you reading this may be saying, "I was not born in a castle; I don't think I've ever met a king or a queen in my life, maybe I've watched a few royal weddings on television, but me? — royalty?—NEVER." Maybe some of you acquired the nickname "Daddy's Princess" or heard your Dad referred to as "King of the House," but by no means have you ever seen a throne or a crown, except for maybe on homecoming court in high school.

For me, it was difficult to wrap my head around being a princess, especially since I couldn't really relate to "royal treatment." I grew up in the little town of McKeesport, Pennsylvania — poverty - and crime-stricken, full of people just making it and only a few who greatly succeeded.

I was raised in a single parent home by a woman of God that had to do it ALL on her own. I was the little girl who wouldn't excel in education, according to an elementary school teacher. So the odds were pretty much against me, except for the fact I had a mother who made sure I learned about a man named Jesus. Growing up in church gave me the foundation I needed to know right from wrong, but I never saw it as my golden ticket into ROYALTY, just rules that restricted me. Little did I know, the foundation my mom set for me would break every curse of poverty, neglect, misfortune, defeat, disappointment and self-pity that attempted to shape my life. I am a young lady who sets an example of success in the little town of McKeesport. While brokenness intended to rule my life, I now have a great relationship with my father, and I am a great role model to my siblings. Where mediocrity tried to rule my life, I am the young lady who missed the honor roll one time, graduated with honors, received scholarships to college, attended and completed college and obtained other degrees. You could say I had something like a Cinderella story — Rags to Riches. Not because I overcame the odds that were against me, but because I accepted my royal crown and allowed Jesus to come and be the King of my life.

I understand that many of you reading this have your own Cinderella story. We all have had hurdles in our lives that may have crippled our paths and obstructed our clear visions of a purposeful future. But there is a great gift of salvation you can have that will make every path straight and God's vision for your future clear.

Before proceeding into this book, before you would even be able to grasp the content of this book, it's so important to me that you know Christ as Your Savior and Lord. You can't accept your royal crown if you do not make Jesus the King of your life. If you place your own crown on your head, then you've given yourself control. If you let someone else crown you, you've given them control over you. I once attempted to control my life, and it never worked out as planned. Ever since I allowed God to reign as my King and control me, my life has never been better. Accepting Jesus literally changed my life, and I was made into a new person! It was time to take off those dirty rags and put on my beautiful crown and royal attire. Accepting your royal crown is, in essence, accepting Jesus as your Lord and Savior. Salvation is a beautiful thing– it essentially means every sin you've committed (evil or wrong thing done) has been washed away by the ultimate love and forgiveness of Jesus Christ, who showed this love by dying on a cross, taking your sins as His own, conquering death by rising from the dead to His original throne in heaven with God, Our Father. If you have never accepted Jesus as your Savior or you need to recommit your vows to Him, please say this prayer with me and accept your royal crown:

God, I thank you for sending your son Jesus to die on the cross for my sins. I know I've done wrong, and I've not made you King over my life. I've allowed my own decisions to keep me bound and followed the ways of others, which has led to confusion, disappointment and a life with only a false sense of hope. I've stayed in these rags too long! I receive my salvation and confess with my mouth that Jesus is my Lord and believe in my heart that You raised Jesus from the dead. I receive Your love, forgiveness, grace and mercy in my life. I surrender myself to you. I accept my royal crown. You are my father, You are my King.

Amen

Scripture on Accepting Your Royal Crown:

Romans 10:9-10

"If you confess with your mouth that Jesus is Lord and believe in your heart that God raised him from the dead, you will be saved. For it is by believing in your heart that you are made right with God, and it is by confessing with your mouth that you are saved."

Romans 6:23

"For the wages of sin is death, but the free gift of God is eternal life through Christ Jesus our Lord."

John 3:16

"For God so loved the world, that He gave His only begotten Son that whosoever believes in Him will not perish but have everlasting life."

Chapter 2
My Father is a King

When we accepted our royal crowns, one of the biggest steps we took was acknowledging Jesus as Savior. We realized that we needed to be saved from our evil ways, but we must also realize that we need a King to rule and direct our ways. Now that we're saved and our slates are clean, we should desire every step we take to be pleasing to our King. Believe me, there will be plenty of times when we slip up and take a step, or two or three, in the wrong direction, but the good news is our King is gracious. Just like our parents tend to have mercy on us in certain situations, so does God our Father. It's important you understand that your Heavenly Father is King and what attributes He has as King. I cannot think of a better way to convey this but through scripture. The Bible is full references of God's Kingdom in heaven, His power and authority, His grace and mercy and so much more, which I will share with you now:

Revelation 1:8

"I am the Alpha and the Omega, the Beginning and the End, says the Lord God, He Who is and Who was and Who is to come, the Almighty (the Ruler of all)."

Jeremiah 32:17

"O Sovereign LORD! You made the heavens and earth by your strong hand and powerful arm. Nothing is too hard for you!"

Psalm 147:5

"Our LORD is great and powerful! He understands everything."

Ephesians 2:4-7

"But God is so rich in mercy, and He loved us so much, that even though we were dead because of our sins, He gave us life when He raised Christ from the dead. (It is only by God's grace that you have been saved!) For he raised us from the dead along with Christ and seated us with him in the heavenly realms because we are united with Christ Jesus. So God can point to us in all future ages as examples of the incredible wealth of his grace and kindness toward us, as shown in all he has done for us who are united with Christ Jesus."

John 14:2

"In My Father's house are many mansions; if it were not so, I would have told you. I go to prepare a place for you."

Revelation 12:10

"Now is come salvation, and strength, and the kingdom of our God, and the power of his Christ."

Psalm 103:19

"The LORD has made the heavens his throne; from there he rules over everything."

Psalm 104:1

"O LORD my God, how great you are! You are robed with honor and majesty."

God, our Father, is King. He not only lives in heaven, but He created and rules it. Your Father is sovereign, all–powerful, mighty, strong and full of mercy, honor and majesty. He loves and gives so much that He gave His life for us that we may be united with Him in heaven.

The Bible speaks of God's greatness: how He is robed with honor and majesty, His incredible wealth of grace and kindness, how He's rich in mercy, seated in heavenly realms, maker of heaven and earth, the ruler of all — The KING in the kingdom of God. So if your father is King, what does that make you? A PRINCESS

Chapter 3
Your Royal Inheritance –
A Princess

You, my dear, are a princess. You are special and prized in the sight of your Father. He has had great plans for you from the womb and anxiously awaits for you to complete them. This is your inheritance: to reign as a daughter of the all-powerful, gracious and loving God, King of the heavens and earth. Yes, I know it's hard to believe, but you are royalty!

Just like scripture was the best way to understand that your father is king, I believe it's the best way for you to embrace your royal inheritance. The Bible is full of affirming and confirming words about who you are in Christ. I encourage you to let these words marinate in your heart, mind and soul until you believe it with all of you.

1 Peter 2:9

"But you are a chosen people, a royal priesthood, a holy nation, God's special possession, that you may declare the praises of him who called you out of darkness into his wonderful light."

Isaiah 43:1,4

"Fear not, for I have redeemed you [ransomed you by paying a price instead of leaving you captives]; I have called you by your name; you are Mine...Because you are precious in My sight and honored, and because I love you, I will give men in return for you and peoples in exchange for your life."

Psalm 139:13-14,17

"For you created my inmost being; you knit me together in my mother's womb. I praise you because I am fearfully and wonderfully made; your works are wonderful, I know that full well...How amazing are your thoughts concerning me O God! How vast is the sum of them!"

Psalm 17:8

"Keep me as the apple of your eye; hide me in the shadow of your wings."

1 Peter 3:4

"But let it be the inward adorning and beauty of the hidden person of the heart, with the incorruptible and unfading charm of a gentle and peaceful spirit, which [is not anxious or wrought up, but] is very precious in the sight of God."

Proverbs 31:10

"A capable, intelligent, and virtuous woman--who is he who can find her? She is far more precious than jewels and her value is far above rubies or pearls."

Jeremiah 1:5

"Before I formed you in the womb I knew [and] approved of you [as My chosen instrument], and before you were born I separated and set you apart, consecrating you."

Romans 8:14-15

"For all who are led by the Spirit of God are children of God. So you have not received a spirit that makes you fearful slaves. Instead, you received God's Spirit when he adopted you as his own children. Now we call him, "Abba, Father."

Colossians 3:12

"Put on therefore, as God's elect, holy and beloved, a heart of compassion, kindness, lowliness, meekness, longsuffering."

You are royalty — a daughter to the King. You are God's special possession, chosen, elect, beloved, separated and set apart, His chosen instrument, fearfully and wonderfully made, the apple of His eye, capable, intelligent, virtuous, precious in God's sight — even more precious than jewels. He knew you in your mother's womb, He redeemed you from sin, called you by name because His thoughts are amazing toward you; He loves you so much, and calls you His child. You must take it beyond wanting to feel special, you must know that you are special and will always be special to the Lord.

When someone loves, cares, nurtures, adores, cherishes and esteems you in a manner like this, it's only normal to want to be closer to that person. Their love for you compels you to love them too. You want to know them more and give them the same kind of love they've given you. Your desire to be around this person intensifies; you want to know their heart's desire, you want to please them, grow with them, enjoy their presence, their embrace, the warmth they give your heart — that's exactly how our relationship should be with our Father. A Princess Whispers To Her Father will lead you on the journey to discovering your King, spilling your heart's desires to Him in every effort to become closer to Him.

Webster defines *whisper* (verb) "to speak softly with little or no vibration of the vocal cords especially to avoid being overheard." I would like to redefine the word whisper for you. A whisper is an intimate moment of expression where your heart's desires are communicated to God, simply known as prayer.

In the next chapters, you will find whispers to Your King that express your aspiration to reflect your royal heritage. You will also find honesty moments, in which you can be completely transparent with God and yourself, as well as challenges that will help put your whispers into action. I encourage you to whisper these prayers to God, be completely vulnerable to the King and allow Him to transform and polish you into the beautiful princess He's called you to be. At the end of each whisper and the close of the book, you will also find pages where you can write your own personal whispers to God, which will propel your personal relationship with Christ even further.

I WANT TO KNOW YOU

Lord, I just want to be close to you. It's an area of the unknown and unusual, but I'm ready to embrace it. I know that as I become closer to you, my life will make more sense, your plan for me will grow clearer, my love for you will grow deeper, and my relationship with you will grow stronger.

"Come near to God and he will come near to you." James 4:8

Honesty Moment: What things are you currently embracing that may prevent you from fully embracing Christ?

Challenge: Whisper to God, then make a list of things you need to let go of and what you need to embrace. Set goals that will strengthen your relationship with Christ(e.g., daily bible reading, morning prayer time, etc.).

Notes: _____

_____

_____

_____

I WANT TO SEEK YOU

Lord, no matter how close we become, I always feel like there's more to you, like a never-ending treasure hunt. I never want to become complacent or comfortable with life or so frustrated and weary in my hard times that I give up and stop seeking you. I seek you as an overall goal in life. I want to know you more, I seek you in everyday life for direction, wisdom, patience and so much more. When I continually seek you, it's hard to lose focus of you. You are my focus — the source of my existence, my reason for living, why I am who I am.

"Seek the Kingdom of God above all else, and live righteously, and he will give you everything you need." Matthew 6:33

Honesty Moment: What causes you to lose focus? What are three main things that occupy your focus/time?

Challenge: Start a three week challenge. Each week, give up one of the things that occupy your time, and replace it with a God-driven focus (e.g., Television occupies my time, so for a week, I use my television time to pray for my family.

Notes: _____

_____

_____

_____

I WANT TO PLEASE YOU

Lord, my heart's desire is to please you. I can honestly say that sometimes, my self-will wants to do opposite of what pleases you, but the very core of me wants to make you proud. I want my life to be one you can use as an example. I don't want my focus to be on pleasing my family, friends, my boss, a man but only you.

"Therefore, I urge you, brothers and sisters, in view of God's mercy, to offer your bodies as a living sacrifice, holy and pleasing to God—this is your true and proper worship." Romans 12:1

Honesty Moment: Who have you been aiming to please (job, family, spouse, etc.)? How has it been working out for you?

Challenge: The next time you're presented with a decision to follow your own or others' will, take a few moments — pray to God, search the Bible to see what God's will is and determine if it lines up with your own/others'.

Notes: _____

_____

_____

_____

I WANT TO BE FAITHFUL

Lord, I want to remain faithful to you. Just thinking of how faithful you've been to me, you never gave up on me when I turned away. You continued to love me even when I disowned you; it compels me to want to be faithful to you. I want to follow your Word, remain consistent in everything that enhances our relationship like prayer, ministry, fasting, bible reading, etc. I want to be faithful and trust you even when I don't understand or can't make sense of the situation. I want to be devoted to you—faithful in love always because you are beyond faithful to me.

"Be faithful until death, and I will give you the crown of life."
Revelation 2:20

Honesty Moment: In what ways have you been unfaithful to God? What can you do to make sure it doesn't happen again? What areas can you be more consistent in?

Challenge: Write your whispers of how unfaithfulness hindered you but how you will allow God's faithful ways to inspire you. Research and memorize a verse about God's faithfulness that inspires you the most.

Notes: _____

_____

_____

_____

I WANT YOUR LOVE

Lord, there is no greater love than Your love. You love without end — through all things, never wavering, always pouring it out on me. Your love compels me to do and live better. I want to love like You so people can come to know You by the love shown through me. I don't want to give an unpredictable, inconsistent, conditional or solely emotionally-driven love to anyone, but I want to display the everlasting, genuine and faithful love of You. Show me and teach me how to love like You.

"No one has greater love [no one has shown stronger affection] than to lay down (give up) his own life for his friends." John 15:13

"Love is patient and kind. Love is not jealous, it does not brag, and it is not proud. Love is not rude, is not selfish, and does not get upset with others. Love does not count up wrongs that have been done. Love takes no pleasure in evil but rejoices over the truth. Love patiently accepts all things. It always trusts, always hopes, and always endures." 1 Corinthians 13:4-7

Honesty Moment: In what areas is your love lacking? (e.g., Your love is kind but not patient and sometimes jealous).

Challenge: Whoever is close to you who you find hardest to love, practice loving them as Your King loves you. Study 1 Corinthians 13, list the areas of love you need the most work on, and practice them on that person.

Notes: _____

_____

_____

_____

I WANT TO SERVE YOU WITH ALL OF ME

Lord, I don't want to serve you with some of me, when I feel like it or when it's convenient, but I want to serve you with all of me. You served us with all of you when you came to Earth, suffered, died on the cross and conquered death, and I want to serve you the same. No regrets, no reserves, no limitations—just a heart, mind and will to give you all of me. I know at times, I may not want to do what I have or need to do, but help me to serve you from a pure heart without complaining but with every part of me.

"...A woman who is not married or a girl who has never married is busy with the Lord's work. She wants to be holy in body and spirit..." 1 Corinthians 7:34

"Servants don't deserve special thanks for doing what they are supposed to do. And that's how it should be with you. When you've done all you should, then say, "We are merely servants, and we have simply done our duty." Luke 17:9-10

"... Behold the handmaid of the Lord; be it unto me according to thy word..." Luke 1:38

Honesty Moment: What regrets, reserves or limitations do you have?

Challenge: Whisper to God your desire to release the regrets and what you'll do to serve Him with all of you. Choose a ministry at your church or a non-profit organization to get involved with, and practice serving with purpose and without complaining as Christ did.

Notes: _____

_____

_____

_____

I WANT TO TRUST YOU

Lord, before you came into my life, trusting others was hard. A life full of disappointments, failed expectations and a bruised heart left me trusting very few people. But now I know you—you have never let me down! I'm learning to trust you and have faith that You'd never lead me astray or leave my life in confusion as it was before. I want my faith and trust in you to increase to the point that I never stagger at Your great and awesome capabilities.

"He staggered not at the promise of God through unbelief, but was strong in faith, giving glory to God." Romans 4:20

Honesty Moment: Who has disappointed you by betraying your trust? What has happened to cause you to stumble or stagger before reaching one of God's promises to You (e.g., fear of failing, critical words from a loved one, etc.).

Challenge: Write a letter to the person who betrayed your trust — express how you felt as well as how you've forgiven and chosen to love them despite what happened. (You don't have to give it to them unless you're compelled to; it's the act of release that's most important). Whisper to God how you will not allow those stumbling blocks to get in your way. Study scripture that will help you overcome the obstacles (e.g., "God has not given me a spirit of fear…" 2 Timothy 1: 7).

Notes: _____

_____

_____

_____

I WANT TO UNDERSTAND YOU

Lord, Your Word, Your revelation, Your voice have all become familiar to me. But I just don't want to know scripture or Your voice, I want to understand you. I've learned the greater my understanding, whether simple or complex, the easier it is for me to activate and apply it to my life. I believe that as I know and understand you more, I can draw more people to salvation, which is my life's desire. I know I'll never understand everything, but fill my cup with as much as I can handle so I can bring you honor.

"Blessed is the man who finds wisdom, And the man who gains understanding." Proverbs 3:13

"Trust in the Lord with all your heart; do not depend on your own understanding. Seek his will in all you do, and he will show you which path to take. Don't be impressed with your own wisdom. Instead, fear the Lord and turn away from evil." Proverbs 3:5-7

Honesty Moment: Do you find yourself putting more trust or finding more security in your own understanding? If so, how often?

Challenge: Whisper to God what you will do to ensure you get His understanding and direction before following your own. Memorize Proverbs 3:5-7.

Notes: _____

_____

_____

_____

I WANT TO FOLLOW YOU

Lord, you have prepared a path for me, you've given me the Bible to help me walk on that path and the Holy Spirit to guide me along the way. I've followed the world's, my family and friends', the enemy's and even my own path for too long. I want to follow you as if my life depends on it, for surely it does. No more chasing unfulfilling, temporal, selfish desires, but I want to follow your will, way, laws and most importantly—your heart. I know that if I follow You, I will lead those that follow me to You.

"There is a way which seems right to a man and appears straight before him, but at the end of it is the way of death." Proverbs 14:12

"The sheep that are My own hear and are listening to My voice; and I know them, and they follow Me." John 10:27

Honesty Moment: What unfulfilling, temporal and selfish desires do you have? What do you think following Christ consists of?

Challenge: List those selfish desires and how you plan to get them out of your life. Find an accountability partner, someone who you trust and can be transparent with, and share your plan with them so they can ensure you follow it.

Notes: _____

_____

_____

_____

I WANT TO SUBMIT AND SURRENDER TO YOU

Lord, surrendering has been an issue for me, especially when for years I thought I had it all under control. The thought of laying down those ways I had worked hard to perfect or cope with flooded me with anxiety. But Lord, I see that these ways that I've adapted to and controlled aren't the best for me; they've left me with a lot of pride, hoarded emotions and wounds that never healed. But as you began to strip me of those familiar ways, a weight was lifted and my outlook changed. As I submit and surrender myself to You, You renew me. I never want this process to end. I'll never be perfect, but I want to always stay surrendered and submitted to You.

"Do not conform to the pattern of this world, but be transformed by the renewing of your mind. Then you will be able to test and approve what God's will is—his good, pleasing and perfect will." Romans 12:2

"So give yourselves completely to God. Stand against the devil, and the devil will run from you." James 4:7

"Casting the whole of your care [all your anxieties, all your worries, all your concerns, once and for all] on Him, for He cares for you affectionately and cares about you watchfully." 1 Peter 5:6-8

Honesty Moment: Do you get in the way of God's plan or hold onto something you need to let go of? What in your life needs to bow down to God? What are you controlling that will be better in His care?

Challenge: Whisper to God your desire to relinquish all control to Him. Write your vows to submit to the King, and place it somewhere that will consistently remind you of the promise you made to God.

Notes: _____

_____

_____

_____

I WANT TO SACRIFICE FOR YOU

Lord, there has been no greater sacrifice than that of Jesus Christ. I understand the magnitude of the ultimate sacrifice, which has given me eternal life. I can never measure up with Your sacrifice, but I want to give You all of me. Even in times when my own way seems more desirable, I want to sacrifice my desire so I can fulfill Yours. Giving You me is the least I can do in return for You saving my life. I don't want to only receive from You, but Lord, let me give back to You.

"Love the Lord your God with all your heart, all your soul, and all your strength." Deuteronomy 6:5

"Then Jesus said to His disciples, If anyone desires to be My disciple, let him deny himself [disregard, lose sight of, and forget himself and his own interests] and take up his cross and follow Me [cleave steadfastly to Me, conform wholly to My example in living and, if need be, in dying, also]." Matthew 16:24

Honesty Moment: Do you give to God, receive more from Him or are you about even? What can you sacrifice more of? (e.g., time in prayer, support in church, etc.).

Challenge: Whisper to God, and list what He has given you and what you've given Him over the past few years. Choose to do something more that will challenge you (e.g., one and a half hour of bible reading as opposed to a half hour); commit to it, and sacrifice to God.

Notes: _____

_____

_____

_____

I WANT TO COMMIT TO YOU

Lord, I want to commit to you. When you've been in unstable relationships filled with broken promises, it's hard to commit fully again. Even after I committed my life to You, the hurt from my past and fear of fully surrendering to You was tough. But once I decided to give You my all and pledge myself totally to You, my life has not been the same. I don't want my past experiences to block me from all You have planned for me. I want to continue to commit everything I do to You for You've always been committed to me.

"Commit your way to the Lord, Trust also in Him, And He shall bring it to pass." Psalm 37:5

"Lord of hosts, blessed (happy, fortunate, to be envied) is the man who trusts in You [leaning and believing on You, committing all and confidently looking to You, and that without fear or misgiving]!" Psalm 84:12

Honesty Moment: What in your past (e.g., relationships, experiences, people, etc.) are blocking you from committing to God? How can you move forward from these things?

Challenge: Whisper to God how you won't allow your past to control your future. Make a daily, weekly and monthly commitment to God (e.g., daily decree, weekly hospital visits, monthly service project, etc.).

Notes: _____

_____

_____

_____

I WANT TO LIVE HOLY FOR YOU

Lord, I want to live holy and righteous for You. I don't want a life that reflects my old ways or even the current ways of this world we live in, but I want a life reflective of You — holy, righteous and pure. There's a lot of pressure to live in a holy life, yet there seems to be very few Christians that hold a standard or drastically change once they accept Your salvation. I want to set and meet a standard that is pleasing to You. If I live my life holy, I know I can influence and encourage others that a holy life is attainable through You.

"I am the LORD your God, and you must dedicate yourselves to me and be holy, just as I am holy." Leviticus 11:44

"Even as [in His love] He chose us [actually picked us out for Himself as His own] in Christ before the foundation of the world, that we should be holy (consecrated and set apart for Him) and blameless in His sight, even above reproach, before Him in love." Ephesians 1:4

Honesty Moment: What do you think of when you hear the word holy? What does it mean to you? Do you feel like your life lines up with your perception and what the scriptures say?

Challenge: List your standards as God's princess for your ministry, relationships, friendships, career, life, family, etc.

Notes: _____

_____

_____

_____

I WANT TO BE INTIMATE WITH YOU

Lord, I've never been flooded with so much passion, love, comfort, concern, attentiveness and sacred moments in my life like I've experienced with You. I want our relationship to go deeper— I want to know Your secrets, what's on Your heart, what brings You joy, what hurts You. I want to learn how to love You more and to love You the way You want to be loved, how to better please You and how to make the most of us. I love Your presence and my time with You. I will always chase intimacy with You because it keeps us connected on a level no one else can relate to or share with us. You're the object of my affection, and I will forever be in pursuit of your heart.

"Yes, furthermore, I count everything as loss compared to the possession of the priceless privilege (the overwhelming preciousness, the surpassing worth, and supreme advantage) of knowing Christ Jesus my Lord and of progressively becoming more deeply and intimately acquainted with Him [of perceiving and recognizing and understanding Him more fully and clearly." Philippians 3:8

"Everyone who confesses that Jesus is God's Son participates continuously in an intimate relationship with God. We know it so well, we've embraced it heart and soul, this love that comes from God." 1 John 4:16

"Call to Me and I will answer you and show you great and mighty things, fenced in and hidden, which you do not know (do not distinguish and recognize, have knowledge of and understand." Jeremiah 33:3

Honesty Moment: On a scale of 1 to 10 (poor to greatest), how would you rate your relationship with Christ? Do you use the standards of past intimate relationships as a tool to measure your relationship with Christ?

Challenge: Whisper to God the ways that you can push your ranking closer to greater intimacy with Him. Set date nights with you and God, where the goal is to enjoy His presence and get to know Him more.

Notes: _____

_____

_____

_____

I WANT TO HEAR, SEE AND FEEL YOU

Lord, just like my natural senses keep me functional, my spiritual senses are needed for me to operate at my full capacity in You. Sometimes, my vision is blurry and my hearing is faint, even my body and emotions become numb and lifeless, and I struggle when I feel like this. In these times, my hope faints, my destiny seems far away, and my body is weak and weary. But Lord when my spiritual senses are heightened, I can hear, see and feel You even more. My hope is placed fully in You, my destiny seems to be in arms reach, my body thrives off of the joy and peace You give me. I want my senses to be beyond sensitive to You so that I'm always fine-tuned and ready to receive what You are giving and revealing to me.

"But I say walk and live [habitually] in the [Holy] Spirit [responsive to and controlled and guided by the Spirit]; then you will certainly not gratify the cravings and desires of the flesh (of human nature without God)." Galatians 5:16

Honesty Moment: How often do your spiritual senses seem to shut down? What triggers it (e.g., stress on the job, family problems, financial issues, temptation, etc.). What spiritual sense(s) would you say needs developed most?

Challenge: List those things that trigger your spiritual shutdown, then list what you can do to counteract a negative reaction. Start a scripture study on the spiritual sense that needs developed the most (e.g., Hearing — study God's voice, Seeing — study vision).

Notes: _____

_____

_____

_____

YOUR PERSONAL WHISPERS

_____

_____

_____

_____

_____

_____

_____

_____

_____

_____

_____

_____

_____

_____

_____

_____

YOUR PERSONAL WHISPERS

_____

_____

_____

_____

_____

_____

_____

_____

_____

_____

_____

_____

_____

_____

_____

YOUR PERSONAL WHISPERS

_____

_____

_____

_____

_____

_____

_____

_____

_____

_____

_____

_____

_____

_____

_____

_____

YOUR PERSONAL WHISPERS

_____

_____

_____

_____

_____

_____

_____

_____

_____

_____

_____

_____

_____

_____

_____

_____

ABOUT THE AUTHOR

Soleil Meade is fiercely committed to serving and loving people. Through her organization, I Am Handpicked, Meade helps women define a clear, purposeful vision for their life. She guides others, who may be bound spiritually and mentally, through their journey to freedom and a life of success on the other side of the journey. When she is not speaking and mentoring others, she is helping to brand others through graphic design and writing. She holds both a Bachelor of Business/Communication and a secondary degree in Graphic Design. Knowing that God has truly handpicked her for purpose, she says, "Handpicked moments come when you know there's something greater than you working on your behalf. There's a conductor that has been orchestrating the music of your life all these years...an artist behind the beautiful masterpiece you've become."

For more information, feedback, and booking...
 Connect with Soleil at www.iamhandpicked.com
Facebook: Soleil Meade
Twitter: MzHandpicked
Email: soleil@iamhandpicked.com